God's Word CONCERNING: Volume 1

PASTOR E. F. LEDBETTER, JR.

God's Word Concerning: Volume 1

By Pastor E.F. Ledbetter, Jr.

All scripture references used in this text are from the King James Version of the Holy Bible.

ISBN 1-891773-22-0

Printed in the United States of America

Published by
Orman Press Inc.
4200 Sandy Lake Drive
Lithonia, Georgia 30038
(770) 808-0999
(770) 808-1955 (fax)
www.ormanpress.com

God's Word Concerning:
Volume 1

Lessons taught in our Wednesday Night Praise Hour

Pastor E. F. Ledbetter, Jr.

The following lessons were written each week in response to the "Spiritual Appetite" of the members of our Wednesday Night Praise Ministry. This is a ministry that is totally designed to meet the "Present" and "Real" needs of our congregation. Each Wednesday, the members of our study express to the Pastor what they would like to learn. By the guidance of the Holy Spirit, we attempt to meet this challenge. The Lord has been faithful in giving us the spiritual wisdom for which we hunger and thirst.

DEDICATION

To the wonderful people of Greater Mt Hebron Church, whose appetite for learning was the motivation for the lessons that are before you.

To my mother, Mildred Guyton, and my sister, Anita Brooks, whose contributions helped to make this book possible.

To each of my sisters, Cecilia, who is with the Lord, Charlene, Lorraine, Sharon, Patricia, Vanessa and Debra, who is also with the Lord.

To my wife, Lydia, and children, Monyetta, Naomi, Ernesha and EF III, whose lives have helped to shape and season me for the work of the Kingdom.

FOREWORD

One of the many things needed in the field of Christian religion today is the proper interpretation of God's scriptures. Many laymen and even pastors and preachers seek prayerfully to reveal the meaning of the Bible in Bible classes, prayer meetings and all worshipful situations. Yet, even with good intentions, sometimes honest and sincere errors are made. Many attempts are made to correct such mistakes, and one of the main attempts is to read and analyze the renderings of sincere and dedicated pastors, who have studied and devoted themselves to the work of plain Bible interpretation.

Pastor E. F. Ledbetter, Jr. has certainly given himself to the devout study of the Bible. His explanation of the vital issues of the Scripture and the relevance in our lives, will help to give the layman and the leadership the direction that we need in the church today.

You will benefit greatly from the use of these scripture references either as a study guide or enlightenment on questions which the seeking Christian is asking today.

I am thrilled to recommend this effort to you.

L. K. Curry, Pastor Emertitus
Emmanuel Missionary Baptist Church (God With Us)
Chicago, Illinois

Table of Contents

GOD'S WORD CONCERNING: BODY MODIFICATION

Leviticus 19:26-28
Deuteronomy 14:1

The people of God were not to follow in the customs of the people of Egypt. Some of these customs involved cutting of hair and beards that were part of worship dedicated to idols. Other practices were eating raw meat, engaging in the occult or witchcraft, and observing astrology.

Eating of raw meat was idolatrous. It was connected with the worship of pagan Gods. The Old Testament teaches us **"the Life is in the Blood."** God seems to teach us to respect the Blood. Probably by consuming the blood in pagan worship, the idolater thought they would bypass the Blood of the sacrifices that pointed to the Crucifixion of Christ. **To God, this was an abomination**.

Engaging in the occult or witchcraft and observing astrology supposes that there is an intelligence other than God, who knows the future and can lead us and guide us in the right way toward lucky days and away from the unlucky. Again, these were the practices of idolatrous and ungodly people. God's people were to be different.

We should not think of it as being an accident or a coincidence that these commands are included in verse 28, for there are some very clear connections with idolatry, astrology and **Body Modification**.

The Word of God says in Leviticus 19:28 (and also in Deuteronomy 14:1) this body is not to be cut on, or even used as a canvas to create all types of drawings. This is clearly linked to superstitious behaviors.

This process of tattooing involved both techniques of drawing on, piercing and disfiguring of the body. Keep in mind the pain that is self-inflicted (which is against nature) (see Mark 5:5); the unsanitary conditions in which these techniques are performed; the permanence of such techniques that until recently would be cut and drawn into the skin forever; names of past loves, ships, aircraft; pictures of animals; artistic work of a sexual nature, or seemingly innocent pictures placed in suggestive areas.

Remember that God created, made and designed our bodies; and to attempt to redesign them for other than that which is necessary for health or life purposes is an insult to our God.

I think I Peter 3:3-4 offers us the conclusion of the whole matter.

GOD'S WORD CONCERNING: "PROPHETS VS. PSYCHICS" Part I

I. What Is a Psychic? By Who's Authority Do They Speak?

When I was a child, they used to call this profession fortunetelling. Theirs is the practice of predicting future events by methods generally considered illogical and unscientific. Some fortunetellers or psychics say that they have powers of clairvoyance–knowledge of future events without using any known senses. The ancient Greeks and Romans believed that God spoke to them through prophets that they called Oracles. Fortunetelling later became astrology, and now is called psychic readings.

The source of their knowledge of future events usually comes from various systems: the sun, the stars, the moon and the planets. In **Numerology**, the fortuneteller or psychic suggests that one's name and birthdate can tell them a lot about their personal future. In **Palmistry**, the psychic supposes to foretell the future by reading lines in ones palm. Some do an investigation before scheduling an interview with a seeker. Some simply know what people want to hear and rely upon expressions of joy and sorrow in the seeker to know whether they are on target or not.

Not only have many people lost great sums of money, but also, because of all of these forces and celestial bodies and a host of superstitious beliefs, people have been robbed of the belief they have the ability to make good decisions based on sound judgment and truth.

King Saul went to a psychic when the Lord refused to answer him. *(I SamueL 28:6-25; Ezekiel 3:1-9, 16, 23; II Kings 21:5-7)*

There is a pursuit for a non-theistic spirituality in the world today. These are some related articles that you should look up:

Astrology	*Magic*	*Omen*
Augur	*Necromancy*	*Oracles*
Clairvoyance	*Nostradamus*	*Palmistry*
Divination	*Numerology*	*Superstition*
Graphology	*Familiar Spirit*	*Occult*

II. What Is a Prophet? By Who's Authority Do They Speak?

A prophet is one who is divinely inspired to communicate God's will to his people, and to disclose the future to them. It was his task also to show the people of God their transgressions. Prophets were the Watchmen of the Old Testament.

II Peter 1:21 says, **"For the prophecy came not of old time by the will of man: but holy men of God spake as they were moved by the Holy Ghost."**

Jeremiah 23:16 says, **"Thus saith the Lord of hosts (now that's where we need to begin!), Hearken not unto the words of the prophets that prophesy unto you: they make you vain: they speak a vision of their own heart, and not out of the mouth of the Lord."**

Old Testament Prophet: Foreteller: exilic, pre-exilic, post-exilic.

New Testament Prophet: Fortuneteller: Pre-written Word.

How does it help us to know things in advance?

1) Knowledge of the future gives us Encouragement. *(from the source)*
2) Knowledge of the future gives us Warning. *(by the source)*

3) Knowledge of the future gives us <u>Faith</u>.
(in the source)

Dr. Unger says that *"Prophecy was not intended to open the future to idle curiosity, but for the higher purpose of furnishing light to those whose faith needs confirming."*

The Prophet and his message were actually another means that God used to reveal his Glory to mere man who has no idea what the future, not even the next second shall bring.

Prophets were never seen as crystal ball gazers, tarot card readers, palm readers, tealeaf readers, stargazers, or planetary prognosticators. They spoke on behalf of God! And, in most cases, it was concerning the will of God pertaining to a Nation, a Kingdom, or the Church.

<u>Examples of Biblical Prophecy</u>

1) The Virgin Birth–Faith.
(Genesis 3:15, Isaiah 7:14)

2) The Wheat and Barley for a Penny - Encouragement, Warning, and Faith. *(II Kings 7:1-20)*

3) Belshazzar's Feast–Faith, Warning. *(Daniel 5:1-31)*

4) The Name of Jesus–Faith, Encouragement.
(Isaiah 7:14, Matthew 1:23)

5) The Birthplace of Christ–Faith, Encouragement. *(Micah 5:2)*

6) The Crucifixion–Faith. *(Isaiah 53)*

7) The Resurrection–Faith. *(John 2:19)*

In conclusion, I believe Proverbs 3:6 gives us the best advice: “In all thy ways acknowledge him, and he shall direct thy paths.”

GOD'S WORD CONCERNING: "PROPHETS VS. PSYCHICS" Part II

The Apostles and the Prophets were Foundational Ministries to the Church. *(Ephesians 2:20)*

God, at this time, speaks through his Son Jesus Christ. *(Hebrews 1:1-3)*

Peter implies that Prophets in the time of his writings were few and diminishing. *(I Peter 2:1)*

We must remember that the office of the **Priest** and **Prophet** operate in the believer. By prayer we operate as priest, and by continued humble study we operate as prophets. Also, you don't have to be a "prophet" to be used of God in conjunction with the **"Gift of Prophecy."** God now works through the **"Body of Christ,"** not through special people as he did in the Old Testament.

Apostles

Acts 1:21-22, 25 gives us the definition of an Apostle.

The Bible is the "Last Word" from God!

1) II Peter 1:20-21
2) II Timothy 3:16-17
3) Hebrews 1:1-2

Isn't it strange that **not one of the New Testament writers** was ever called a Prophet?

Do Apostles and Prophets still exist?

Paul only gives direction on the criteria for a Bishop and a Deacon. And he encourages Timothy to do the work of an Evangelist. *(II Timothy 4:5, I Timothy 3, Titus 1:6-16)*

In some of the New Testament letters, saints, brethren, and elders are recognized. In the letter to Philippi, Paul even addresses the **Bishops** and **Deacons** in verse 1.

<u>Why didn't he salute the "Prophets" if they still exist?</u>

GOD'S WORD CONCERNING: "THE CASE OF BRO. SAINT VS. BRO. SAINT"

I Corinthian 6:1-20

The Law of God: The Ten Commandments & The Mosaic Law *(Exodus 19:20)*

The best place to begin this lesson is with the Law of God, because it is God who has the power to enlighten us as to what is truly wrong, or sinful.

Now, the Ten Commandments were quite brief and fundamental. The purpose for which they were given was to deprogram the Israelites who had just made their Exodus from Egypt. After more than 400 years of bondage these people had become compromised by the customs and the traditions of the Egyptians. If they were to truly be a sanctified people, they needed to be separated in the heart as well as in the Land!

In order to give explanation to the Law of God, Moses wrote a breakdown of the law that focused on every day situations, such as **proper diet, holy sexuality, sacrifices, hygiene, proper social behavior, and much more!**

The penalty of violating the Law of God in many cases meant very simply, **death.** In many cases the basic rule was an eye for an eye, a tooth for a tooth, and a life for a life. I'm sure that you can see how this type of severity kept the rate of crime in pretty good order.

Now in the New Testament Jesus says that trouble is inevitable (see Matthew18:7).

Matthew 18 teaches us to have the utmost respect and reverence for the rights of life for the least among us, and verses 15 - 20 offer rules for dealing gracefully with offenses.

Matthew 19:28 also sheds light on why we need to really learn how to handle problems in this world, because there is a greater honor and responsibility coming later. We're being prepared for Judgment positions!

You see, if we are faithful over a few things here, we have been promised the responsibility of being rulers over many in glory. *(Matthew 25:21-23)*

Finally, this brings us to **I Corinthians Chapter 6**, where obviously the Church was being made to **look foolish** by many who had problems with one another and didn't know how to deal with them in a **Christ-like way.**

The Apostle Paul teaches them that they ought to be saved enough and wise enough to handle their own problems without allowing unsaved people to be placed in authority over Christians who ought to be in position to set standards and examples for the world.

GOD'S WORD CONCERNING: NINE GIFTS OF THE SPIRIT

I Corinthians 12:1-11

<u>**Gifts of Revelation**</u> Mind
Three Gifts that Reveal Something!

1) The Gift of the Word of Wisdom–<u>Future</u>

2) The Gift of the Word of Knowledge–<u>Present & Past</u>

3) The Gift of Discerning of Spirits–<u>Divine Insight</u>

<u>**Gifts of Power**</u>
Three Gifts That Do Something!

4) The Gift of Faith

5) The Gift of Working Miracles

6) The Gifts of Healing

The working of miracles is the gift of miracles, but the receiving of a miracle is the gift of faith.

<u>**Gifts of Inspiration**</u> (utterance) Vocal
Three Gifts That Say Something!

7) The Gift of Prophecy

8) The Gift of Divers Kinds of Tongues

9) The Gift of Interpretation of Tongues
Tongues + Interpretation = Prophecy

Prophesying, Preaching, and Prophets are three distinctly different ministries or functions.

"Let All Things Be Done Decently and in Order"
(I Corinthians 14:40)

1) <u>The Gift of the Word of Wisdom</u>

The word of wisdom is a supernatural revelation by the Holy Spirit concerning the divine purpose in the mind and the will of God. On the Isle of Patmos (Revelation 1:1-4), John exhibits both the word of wisdom and the word of knowledge.

2)<u>The Gift of the Word of Knowledge</u>

The word of knowledge is the supernatural revelation by the Holy Spirit of certain facts in the mind of God. *(See Acts 9:10-12, Acts 10:9-20; II King 6:9-12; II Kings 5:25, 26.)*

3)<u>The Gift of Discerning of Spirits</u>

The discerning of spirits gives insight into the spirit world *(Acts 16:16-18, Romans 8:14).*

4)<u>The Gift of Faith</u>

Those who possess the gift of faith believe God in such a way that He honors their word as His own, and He miraculously brings it to pass.

Wisdom/Faith/Miracles *(I Kings 17:1)*
There is Saving Faith *(Ephesians 2:8)*

There is General Faith *(Romans 12:3)*
There is the Fruit of Faith *(Galatians 5:22-23)*
There is the Gift of Faith *(I Corinthians 9)*

5)<u>The Gift of Miracles</u>

A Miracle is a supernatural intervention in the ordinary course of nature; a temporary suspension of the accustomed order through the Spirit of God.

Acts 27 shows Paul in a storm with the gift of faith.
Mark 4:39 shows Jesus in a storm with the gift of miracles.

6) <u>The Gifts of Healing</u>

The purpose of the gifts of healing is to deliver the sick and to destroy the works of the devil in the human body. *(Acts 10:38, Luke. 4:18)*

7) <u>The Gift of Prophecy</u>

I Corinthians 14:1-5, Acts 21:8-11, and Acts 2:10-11 reveal the word of wisdom working with the gift of prophecy.

8) <u>The Gift of Tongues</u>

Divers kinds of tongues is the supernatural utterance by the Holy Spirit in languages never learned and not necessarily understood by the speaker or the hearer.
(Mark 16:15-18, I Corinthians 14:27-28)

9) <u>The Gift of Interpretation of Tongues</u>

The interpretation of tongues is the supernatural showing forth by the

Holy Spirit the meaning of an utterance in other tongues. Note: not the translation of tongues but the interpretation! *(I Corinthians 14:13-15, 27, 28, 40)*

GOD'S WORD CONCERNING: HOW ETERNAL IS MY SECURITY?

The next subject we will embark upon is also known as "The Doctrine of Eternal Security," but it is best known as "Once Saved Always Saved."

As I researched in an attempt to prepare myself for this lesson, I discovered some very important things that I'm sure we will all benefit from.

Here are some very thought provoking questions that you and I need to ask ourselves:

1. Does each act of sin jeopardize my **Salvation**?
2. Whose hand is my **Salvation** in, **Mine** or the **Lord's**?
3. Will God "**Keep**" me against "**My**" will?
4. Does God treat **Sons** and **Daughters** the same as **Strangers**?
5. Do I need to be **Rebaptised** when I sin?
6. Does the Bible teach that the **Backslider** is Lost?

While pondering those questions, answer these:

1. *What is a Believer?*
2. *What is a Backslider?*
3. *What is an Apostate?*

I. The Bible teaches that the **Love of God saved us in spite of Sin.**

   A. Receiving this makes us a Believer.
   B. The Believer's **heart and life** is turned toward God.
   C. The Believer is Saved and in right relationship.

II. The Bible teaches that, although we've been saved, there are those who **"slide back"; but there is still hope of return**!

A. Knowing this and falling into a lifestyle of sin makes us a Backslider.
B. The Backslider's **heart is turned toward God**, but his **life is turned to the world**.
C. The Backslider is saved, **without reward**, and **not in right relationship.**

III. The Bible teaches that, although we've been saved, there are those who **slide back** and become **hardened in sin** and **never return**!

A. Knowing this and falling into a lifestyle of sin and rejecting God's invitation to return makes one an **Apostate.**

B. The Apostate's heart and life have not only turned, but have gone into rejection.

Let us look at some examples of Backsliders in the Word of God: Psalm 51; Matthew 26:70-75; Luke 23:31-34; John 21:15-17; I Corinthians 5; and II Corinthians 2.

Did you know that God is married to the backslider? *(Jeremiah 3:14-22, 4:1)*

1. Though backslidden, the Love of God remains in tact.

2. Though backslidden, the marriage is still in tact.

3. Though backslidden, the benefits would still be in tact and are available if the relationship is restored.

The word "keep" comes from the Greek word TEREO–a fortress, to watch over, to preserve.

God the Father, God the Son, and God the Holy Ghost "keep" the Believer. *(John 14, John 15, John 17:11-12)* Jesus says that those who are in the hands of the Father are saved eternally! *(John 10:28-29)*

The Apostle Paul says God Loved us before we were Saved.
(Romans 5:8)

The Apostle Paul also says that nothing can sever us from the Love of God. (Romans 8:34-39)

God has the power to "KEEP" those who want to be KEPT!
(II Timothy 1:12)

David implies that he realizes that though he has sinned he's not yet a **castaway**. He would become one if he doesn't **repent**! *(Psalm 51:11)*

God can remove whole churches from His presence.
(Revelation 2:5)

God will stay with you, if you remain with him.
(II Chronicles 15:2)

<u>More:</u>
I Timothy 4:1, Galatians 1:6-8, 5:4, II Peter 2:20-22,
I Timothy 1:19, Hebrews 6:4-9, Hebrews 10:26-29,
Deuteronomy 29:18-21, and don't forget the Book of Hosea.

Notice how God works with sets of threes:
Peter denied Christ three times
Peter's restoration was three-fold

The ways into the church are:
(i) Candidate for baptism
(ii) Christian experience
(ii) Letter from a church of like faith

The Spiritual Man	*The Believer*
The Carnal Man	*The Backslider*
The Natural Man	*The Apostate*

One on the Rise in Faith! ***One on the Fall into Apostasy!***

GOD'S WORD CONCERNING:
MORE THAN SAVED!

This is a strange topic until you realize that there is more to being saved in regard to our forthcoming rewards, than just being saved. You can actually be "More Than Saved."

Now, it's difficult to discuss this subject without first stating that there are actually five Judgments and three Thrones in Scripture. Here they are:

TIME	PLACE	SUBJECT	BASIS	RESULT
A.D. 30 10:4 ROMANS 10:4 (PAST)	CALVARY	SIN	CHRIST'S FINISHED WORK	1. DEATH TO CHRIST 2. JUSTIFICATION TO THE REWARD OR LOST
AFTER THE RAPTURE 2COR. 5:10	BEMA OR JUDGMENT SEAT OF CHRIST	BELIEVERS AS TO THEIR WORKS	THEIR WORKS	
GREAT TRIBULATION MAT. 24:21-31	JERUSALEM & VICINITY	JEWS	REJECTION OF GODHEAD	CONVERSION AND RECEPTION OF CHRIST
REVELATION OF CHRIST MAT. 25:31-46 (FUTURE)	THE THRONE OF HIS GLORY	THE NATIONS	THE TREATMENT OF THE BRETHREN OF JESUS	SOME SAVED AND SOME LOST
RENOVATION BY FIRE REV. 20:11-15	THE GREAT WHITE THRONE	THE WICKED	THEIR WORKS	CAST INTO THE LAKE OF FIRE.

THE THREE THRONES

THRONE	TEXT	PLACE	CONCERNING
The Judgment Seat of Christ	2 Cor. 5:10Seat	In the Air	For Believers Only
The Throne of Glory	Matt. 25:31-32	On the Earth"	For the Nations
The Great White Throne	Rev. 20:11-12	In Heaven	For the Wicked

The Believer is Judged on Three Levels

1. As a **Sinner** in the past. *(I John 2:1/I John 1:9)*

2. As a **Son** in the present. *(John 5:24)*

3. As a **Servant** in the future. *(I Corinthians 11:31-32)*

The Five Crowns

1. The Crown of Life *(James 1:12, Revelation 2:10)*
2. The Crown of Rejoicing *(I Thessalonians 2:19-20, Philippians 4:1)*
3. The Crown of Righteousness *(II Timothy 4:8)*
4. The Crown of Incorruptible *(I Corinthians 9:25-27)*
5. The Crown of Glory *(I Peter 5:2-4)*

Judgment of Believer's Works *(I Corinthians 3:12-15)*

This Judgment is not a Judgment to determine whether one is saved or lost. This one is to determine the degree of reward one will receive. The very fact of one's presence at this Judgment suggests that the particular person is saved.

<u>Notice that there are six levels of works for which each believer will be judged:</u>

1. **Gold** (representing the highest level or quality of works)
2. **Silver**
3. **Precious Stones**
4. **Wood**
5. **Hay**
6. **Stubble** (representing the lowest level or quality of works)

Christian Ministry that seeks to **win the Lost** and **proclaim the Name of Jesus** is represented by the category of <u>Gold, Silver, and Precious Stones</u>.

Christian Ministry that may have been h**elpful** and even **sincere**, but only **temporary** at best is represented by the category of <u>Wood, Hay, or Stubble</u>.

The authenticity of all our works will be tested by fire. If they are truly spiritual they will last. If they are not they will not endure the test of fire. It's possible for one's house to be lost and his life be saved. Some will escape this judgment and be **"<u>More Than Saved.</u>"**

GOD'S WORD CONCERNING: THE SIGNS OF THE TIMES

Three Great Questions ???

1. *When shall these things be?*
2. *What shall be the signs of thy coming?*
3. *What shall be the signs of the end of the world?*

The purpose of this lesson is to help us understand that Christ has given the believer enough information to be aware of what will come to pass. We are not told exactly when, but we are only given these various "Signs of the Times."

It is very important to remember that the Book of Matthew was written to the Jews to remind them that Jesus is the King, and also to remind them of what is ahead for those who rebel or receive His Kingdom.

Whenever signs are given, they are for the purpose of causing faith to develop. Many times we are not able to describe these things specifically. But as we read the Bible in one hand and the newspaper in the other, we begin to discern the prophetic mind of the Lord.

Just as in the days of Belshazzar, who, because of his irreverence to God, saw fingers of a man's hand, the handwriting is on the wall. Signs of the Lord's second coming are everywhere.

Let's Look at Matthew 24

I. The Destruction of Jerusalem
II. The Tribulation: The First half (3 1/2 years)
III. The Tribulation: The Second half (3 1/2 years)
IV. The Second Coming

I. The Destruction of Jerusalem

A. Jerusalem completely encircled by armies–Luke 21:20-24

B. The Temple leveled down to the last stone.

C. Her people will be killed and some led captive into all nations.

D. Jerusalem will be trodden down by the Gentiles until the time of the fullness of the Gentiles be fulfilled. Note: It is clear that the Lord is speaking of two separate destructions.

1. The Historical Destruction, by Titus on Sept 8th 70 AD. Supposedly a rumor, that real gold was used to hold the marble blocks together,caused the soldiers to literally tear each stone apart from one another in order to find riches.

2. The 2nd Destruction is to take place some time during the Great Tribulation.

Incidentally, the saints at this time will be in Heaven at the Bema Seat of Christ and the Marriage Supper of the Lamb.

II. The Tribulation: The First Half (3 1/2 years) *(Matthew 24:3-14, 10:17-23; Mark 13:4-13; Luke 21:7-19, 12:11-12)*

A. False prophets and messiahs will arise and deceive many.

B. Wars and rumors of wars will intensify. (The United Nations is constantly resolving global problems.)

C. Famines, Pestilence, Earthquakes, and Great Signs in the Heavens. (Germ Warfare)

D. Believers scourged, imprisoned and hated, betrayed even by family.

E. Wickedness multiplied and love devalued into coldness.

III. The Tribulation: The Second Half (3 1/2 years) *(Matthew 24:15-31, 36-42; Mark13:14-27, 32-37; Luke 21:25-28, 34-36)*

A. The Abomination of Desolation will be unveiled in the Temple's Holy of Hollies. (Probably, a statue of the Antichrist.)

B. The world's most severe tribulation and persecution will begin.

C. The sun and the moon will be darkened.

D. The sea will be at the center of much destruction.

E. The hearts of men will experience unprecedented terror.

F. The Battle of Armageddon will take place.

G. Christ will return.

IV. The Second Coming – The saints will be coming with Him from Heaven. ***(Matthew 24:29-41)***

A. His elect are gathered by the angels.

B. The unsuspecting wicked removed and destroyed as in the days of Noah.

The Sermon From the Fig Tree *(Matthew 24:32-34)*

Examples of Signs

1. Religious Warfare

2. Religious Indifference

3. Biological Warfare
(Anthrax, smallpox and ebola, genetically altered bacteria are present concerns in Iraq)

4. Global Chaos

5. Rapid Increase of Knowledge and Technology
(computer technology has changed this world forever)

6. Moral Depravity

7. Terrorism
(Oklahoma and the U.N. are proof of terrorism on American soil)

Warning to Date Setters–Matthew 24:36
Warning to Embrace Readiness–Matthew 24:42-44

Other References

II Thessalonians 2:1 - 17 - Things That Must Happen First.

II Timothy 3:1-13 - Character of the Last Days

II Peter 2:1-22 - The Damnable Doctrines of the Last Days

II Peter 3:1-18 - The Day of the Lord

We must always keep in mind that because we are the "Children of the

Light," God has given us His Word to encourage, inform, and to warn us ahead of time that we would reach the lost and share the same with them. Remember also, that if you are saved now, these things are not meant to frighten you. As a matter of fact, they are only relevant to those who miss the "Rapture."

Therefore, I think it's safe to say "I'll see you in the Rapture."

GOD'S WORD CONCERNING: 3 BUT 1 "THE TRINITY"

Although many denominations disagree, there is undeniable evidence throughout the Bible that though our God is One, He has revealed himself in three Manifestations. They are God the **Father**, God the **Son**, and God the **Holy Ghost**. "Hear oh Israel that the Lord our God is one Lord" *(Deuteronomy 6:4).*

One of the best ways to understand or at least make your way toward understanding is by thinking about water. Although water is one element, in freezing temperatures it becomes ice **(solid)**. In normal temperatures, it remains a **liquid**. In extremely hot temperatures, water becomes a **Gas** that we call steam. All three are still water (H^2O), but manifested in these three different forms.

Now you will not find the word **Trinity** in the Scriptures, but an overwhelming amount of biblical foundation is there to prove that this doctrine is true.

Trinity

I. The Trinity is Quietly Declared in the Old Testament.

A. Genesis 1:1 presents the first reference to the Hebrews name of God that is singular in its beginning and plural in its ending (IM signifies plurality). In the beginning God (Elohim) (also Genesis 1: 26, Genesis 11:7, Isaiah 6:8.)

B. Genesis 22: 11-12 and Exodus 3:1-15 offer what is called theophanies (appearances of God in human form).

C. Isaiah 6:3 says that God is Thrice Holy.

II. The Trinity is Openly Declared in the New Testament.

A. In the Baptism of Christ. Matthew 3:16-17
B. In the formula for Baptism. Matthew 28:19
C. In the teaching of Jesus. John 14:16-17
D. In the fact that all three are called God.
Romans1:7, 9:5, Hebrews 1:8, Acts 5:3-4

- As God the Father, He is **Sovereign.**
- As God the Son, He is **Redeemer.**
- As God the Holy Ghost, He is **Comforter.**

- All three were involved in our Creation.
- All three were involved in our Redemption.
- All three are involved in our Comfort.

Now it ought to be understood that the Father is known or manifested as God, the Son as Redeemer, and the Holy Ghost as the Comforter, the third person of the Godhead. This is the normal order in which they are usually presented, but it is not essential that they be this way in every case.

In other words, there is no inferiority or superiority among the Godhead. Jesus is not subordinate to God, the Holy Ghost is not subordinate to Jesus. God is not superior to either in nature, essence, or being. They are equal. They are one, with equal power, equal attributes, and even equal in existence. And in every way they are equal, infinitely.

They are only subordinate in office, but not in nature. Consider the President and every citizen of the United States. The office of the

President elevates its holder above others, but in reality he is a man as other men are.

The order that we have become accustomed to is really only for the purpose of remaining focused in reference to the Pre-incarnate God, the Father; the Incarnate God, the Son; and the Post-incarnate God–the Holy Ghost.

God the Father was most visible in the Old Testament.
God the Son was most visible between the Testaments.
God the Holy Ghost is most visible in the New Testament.

Because of this, we really need to speak more in reference to what the Holy Ghost is doing in this present dispensation.

Can this be the reason why many miracles are not manifested, as they ought, because we have not truly recognized the member of the Godhead that is presently operating?

<u>Other Scriptures That Declare the Trinity</u>

John 1:1-14
Here, John describes a savior that is co-existent with the Father, who was with him in the beginning, and is one and the same as the Father. And furthermore, that this Word became incarnate (took upon himself flesh).

John 10:30
Here, John's Gospel reveals Jesus describing the inseparable nature of Himself and the Father.

Well, we could go on, but the bottom line is that you don't have to understand it to believe it, just believe it to be saved. "For he that believeth and is baptized shall be saved." *(Mark 16:16*)

GOD'S WORD CONCERNING: AM I HERE ON THE RIGHT DAY?

Saturday, Sunday, Sabbath Day, the Lord's Day, which one is the right one? Was there a change in the calendar? What about Constantine's alleged change on March 7th, 321 A.D.? Did he and the Pope of that day tamper with the calendar to further confuse the issue? What about Blue Laws? Is it equally as wrong to do on Sunday what Sabbath keepers deemed as wrong on the Sabbath? Questions, questions, and more questions, but we need some answers and thank God that through the Word of God we have just what we need.

How It all Began

Even though the Sabbath was first exercised by God in his act of ceasing from creating, the actual institution of a national observance is from the Law of Moses. Exodus 16:23-29.

The Babylonians also observed a series of Sabbaths, but theirs were associated with the stars, the moon, astrological movements, and much more. As a matter of fact, the word "Sabbath" has a Babylonian origin. The Babylonians kept festivals and fasts days on the 7th, the 14th, the 19th, the 21st and the 28th day of each month. Dr. Unger says that this 19th day falls out of sequence and was unexplained.

What Does it Mean?

The Jewish Sabbath had no relation with Babylonian astrology or polytheistic worship. It was a day of rest to reflect upon the completion of a week of labor. I believe it also was a way for the Lord to keep before us, on a weekly basis, what would one day be ours to enjoy each and every day throughout eternity!

Who Did It Affect?

This sanctification of the Seventh Day was given by God to help this sanctified people to be separated, and to live separate from the world. It was a sign of promise between Jehovah and the Children of Israel forever. *(Exodus 31:17)*

What Was to Cease?

There was to be no cooking, no cleaning, no gathering of wood, no trading, and no traveling. The gates of the city in Nehemiah's day were even closed to enforce this.

What Was Done?

Each day of the week a lamb was usually offered, but on the Sabbath Day there would be two. New showbread was to be placed on the Temple Table. Thus, the Day of the Sabbath to Israel was a day of Gladness. *(Numbers 10:10, Hosea 2:11)*

Ezekiel 20:12, 20 reminds us again that it was a sign between Israel and Jehovah that they might know that "I am the Lord that sanctifies" them. The penalty for Sabbath Breakers was death. *(Exodus 31:15, 25:2)*

The Sabbath & The Lord's Day Contrasted

The Sabbath reflects upon Creation Rest.
The Lord's Day reflects upon Resurrection.

The Sabbath reflects upon how God ceased working.
The Lord's Day reflects upon how Christ unceasingly continues.

The Sabbath Day commemorates a Finished Creation.
The Lord's Day commemorates a Finished Redemption.
The Sabbath Day remembers the Old Creation that I was.

The Lord's Day remembers the New Creation that I am.

The Lord's Day

The Lord's Day, the first day of the week, reflects upon the New Creation that we are with Christ himself as the Resurrected Head. This is not simply a changeover of a day, but the marking of a new dispensation.

The Lord's Day offers to believers an entirely new attitude, for with it we have a day of privilege as opposed to the Sabbath Day that comes at the end of a week of labor.

Because it reflects upon the day of our redemption by the resurrection of Christ, the attitude attached to it is to rejoice! (*Matthew 28:9-10*). Because we are saved forever, the spirit of rejoicing can be extended beyond even Sunday to every day of the week. This was something that the Law and the Sabbath could not do. *(Romans 14:5-6)*

Legalism

Legalism is the attempt to gain favor with God based upon the works and accomplishments of righteousness. We are warned that legalism is a backward step. *(Galatians 4:9-10)*

The Law Doesn't Justify *(Galatians 3:11-12)*

The work of Christ at Calvary destroyed every ordinance that was against us and set us free from every form of Bondage. *(Colossians 2:14-17)*

What is the Bottom Line?

The rule of thumb is that the Christian Church is not a continuation of the Nation of Israel. We are the ecclesia, the "Called Out." Therefore, the observances of the Body of Christ are given to us from Christ and are found in the New Testament. With this in mind, there is nowhere in the New Testament that the Body of Christ is commanded to keep a particular day as the Jews did.

Now, we do keep a day, but originally it was done because it meant death if it was not observed. We keep it because through the resurrection of Christ we have received life. We are not the servants of the day. The day is given to serve us. The Son of Man is Lord over the Sabbath. *(Mark 2:27-28)*

Proof of Lord's Day Observances in the New Testament

Pentecost was on the 50th day after the Resurrection, which was a Sunday. *(Acts 2)*

Preaching, and the issuing of the Lord's Supper, was known to be done on the first day of the week. *(Acts 20:7)*

John spoke of being in the Spirit on the Lord's Day. *(Revelation 1:10; also see Matthew 28:1, Mark 16:9; John 20:1, 19, 26; and I Corinthians 16:2)*

GOD'S WORD CONCERNING: "WHERE IN THE WORLD IS HEAVEN?"

Now this study is one that is truly over our heads! You can't begin to talk about heaven without focusing on the sky. The sky is the name given to this great dome of the heavens that we see above us.

The Word of God begins by saying "**In the beginning God created the Heaven and Earth**." *(Genesis 1:1)* Thousands of years ago before modern science and its discoveries, Moses had already received information from God that the sky was a space between the waters above and below.

The Apostle Paul spoke of being ushered into the third heaven. It goes without saying that if there is a third heaven, there must be a first and a second. *(II Corinthians 12:2)*

Now even though when we think of heaven our eyes are usually drawn to the upward way, in the scriptural sense the first heaven begins from the ground up and out. This is where the birds, clouds, rain, wind and snow are found. The second heaven is where the moon, stars and planets reside.

<u>A Word From a Scientific View</u>

Scientist divide the earth's atmosphere into about 4 or 5 layers. They are:

1) The **Troposphere**, approximately 5-7 miles above where the clouds reside.

2) The **Stratosphere,** which is above the clouds 10-60 miles up.

3) The **Ionosphere**, the domain of radio waves. about 18 1/2 miles up.

4) The **Exosphere,** which is all the air above 120 miles.

(There are differing opinions that also include a **Mesosphere** and a **Thermosphere.**)

Now in Hebrew Scripture, heaven, which comes from the word "firmament," appears to be like an arch spread out over the whole earth, supported by pillars and a foundation (II Samuel 22:8, Job 26:11), with rain descending through its windows or gates.

Since the first heaven is occupied by the fowl and the clouds, and the second heaven is the palace of the planets, the moon, and the stars, then the third heaven must be the Throne of God, as well as the place where the angels of God reside. **Exactly where this is isn't revealed**. Even when the Apostle Paul was taken there he was not allowed to tell us where this was or even to describe what he saw. Heaven seems to be a place that is relative to the experience of those who expect to enter. The Eskimo thinks of it as a warm place. The desert dweller thinks of it as being a place where there is shade and the abundance of water. The slave thinks of it as a place of freedom. But most of all it is the capital city of God's Divine Presence.

(It should be mentioned that in recent years even an "Ozonosphere" was discovered and is better known as the "Ozone Layer".)

Now the Good Part!

Although we know the location of the first and the second heaven, the reason why no spaceship or any vehicle of any earthly nature can catapult us there is because the third heaven cannot be received or even perceived in the natural. It is a spiritual place, as real as any place that we know of in this world. *(John 14:1-6)*

At the Rapture We Go to Heaven

Jesus told the disciples that he was the "Way" to heaven, the "Door of the Sheep." Knowing Jesus is the way to heaven. At the rapture, Christ will come to take us (seeing that of ourselves we cannot know the way). Christ will come to take us to the third heaven.

Now during that particular time we will be citizens of heaven for seven years. There we will be occupied with two major activities: the receiving of reward for Christian service, as well as the celebration of the Marriage Supper of the Lamb. *(Revelation 19:1-9)*

After the Celebration We Return to Earth

Matthew 5:5 tells us that the "meek shall inherit the earth." Revelation 19:14 reveals that after the party in heaven, we then will return with Christ to take possession of the earth that we left seven years before. (By the way, this is the Second Coming.) At this time, Revelation 20 describes the nature of the Millennial Kingdom.

No More Grace, But Righteousness

This Kingdom will last for 1000 years. Because the devil, Satan, the deceiver will be bound for that same space of time in the bottomless pit, there will be no temptation, and no sin because of temptation. If any sin, it will be because they so desire. Therefore, the character of this Kingdom will be strictly that of righteousness. *(Revelation 19:15)*

After the Millennial Kingdom, the New Jerusalem Will Come to Us

Revelation 21 begins with the tremendous truth that the old heaven and the old earth would be of no use and that the old would give way to the new.

The New Jerusalem

This new city has gates (for entering and exiting). It has foundations. It has no temple, but this is not to suggest that it won't be a place of worship, for God Almighty and the Lamb shall be its Temple. It needs no sun or moon, for God Almighty and the Lamb shall be the source of its light. The gates never close, therefore we have continued access to it at all times.

It seems to me that what God is going to do in the creation of this new heaven and new earth is not only a process of renovation, but also relocation!

This Relocation of the Holy City, the New Jerusalem, Will Place the Eternal Presence of God Closer to Us Than He Has Ever Been!

GOD'S WORD CONCERNING: "WHAT REALLY HAPPENS WHEN I FAST?"

(Isaiah 58:3-14)

I. The Wrong Reason to Fast (vs. 3-5)

II. The Right Reason to Fast (vs. 6-7)

III The Rewards of a Fast (vs. 8-14)

When I think of "fasting," there seems to be much more than meets the eye. Fasting is more than going without food for a certain period of time.

It must include a separation of all that (though it may not be sinful) and is not of God. It is a time of giving ones self to communion with God. In only a few moments of a fast, one will easily begin to see how far we are from God and also how truly addicted we are to the things of the world. Urges for things that we normally don't desire become like little wars in a vast battlefield of life.

The aroma of fresh brewed coffee, bacon frying in the skillet, and white or wheat bread in the toaster test our endurance in the morning. A candy bar calls to you, or an ice cream cone in the noonday, and driving by a rib joint is like torture in the evening.

But not only that, it seems that this is when your favorite music is on the radio, favorite programs are on the television, and a friend calls or stops by unexpectedly, whose conversations cover a vast potpourri of subjects.

Maybe your children are in the best of moods, your companion looks more attractive than ever, and here you are on a fast.

Now here are some things that may be helpful in accomplishing a successful fast!

1) **<u>Begin, Continue, and End With Prayer!</u>**

Without prayer, you cannot have a successful fast. A separation without prayer is more like a secular diet or weight loss program, or even good behavioral morality. People who are not saved can do these things. Prayer is the other half of the whole of fasting. One part is the turning away from the world; the other is turning to God. Prayer is what makes it consecrated.

2) **<u>Keep Your Goals Clearly in Sight!</u>**

What is the purpose of your fast? Why have you engaged in this? If you are not serious and sincere, you will be defeated before you can get started.

3) **<u>Season it All With Grace!</u>**

There should be nothing legalistic about fasting in the New Testament Church. Legalism is when one attempts to earn salvation by one's works and rituals. Because it is spiritual, it is not a matter of hours or days or even how ascetic one can be. There is nothing magical or mystical about it. It is real and it is holy.

Therefore, allow the Lord to help you to start out small and grow to other levels as you grow in his grace. Jesus fasted forty days. You may not be led of the Spirit to begin here. But it does give you something to work toward. If you fail in mind or body in the process, don't stop! Simply ask for forgiveness and continue on.

In Conclusion

Finally, fasting, at its best, is hard spiritual work. Satan will try to hinder you but Christ will help you. Though the way may get rough and the pressure weighs heavily, press on to the finish line. The rewards are tremendous!

GOD'S WORD CONCERNING: "ANOINTED AND HIGHLY FAVORED OF GOD"

In the Old Testament there were many who were blessed by God to be used in ways that were unavailable to others. Because the Holy Spirit was not come into his "full office," there were "special people" who God wanted to use in "special ways." To accomplish this, "highly favored" persons would be "anointed."

To "anoint" means to pour oil upon as to signify consecration. In Luke 1:28, we find the term "highly favored," which means endued with grace.

Various Anointings

- Aaron was anointed to be High Priest (Exodus 28:41; 29:7; 30:30; 40:13; Psalm 133:2)
- Saul (I Samuel 9:16; 10:1; 15:1) The evil spirit didn't trouble Saul until the Holy Spirit left.
- David (I Samuel 16:3-13; II Samuel 2:4; 5:3)
- Absalom (II Samuel 19:10)
- Solomon (I Kings 1:34-45; 5:1)
- Hazael (I Kings 19:15)
- Elisha (I Kings 19:16)
- Lucifer (Ezekiel 28:14)
- Paul and more (II Corinthians 1:21)
- Many material items were also "anointed" such as:
    - Cakes (Leviticus 7:12)
    - Tabernacle (Exodus 30:26)
    - Vessels (Numbers 7:1)
    - Laver of Brass (Exodus 40:11)

As you engage in study of these and other references on anointings, you will discover that whenever one is anointed, it is always for more than what many think. You see, the anointing is not for the purpose of simply making one happy or even holy. In each case that I have seen, the primary purpose of the "anointing" is for **power and service!**

What About Today?

Now, since the death, burial and resurrection of Christ, no longer is the Holy Spirit reserved for "special people" at "special times." Today, because of Christ, the anointing is not only available, but also **essential**. Jesus commands his disciples to remain in the Upper Room until they are endued with power from on high! *(Acts 1:4)* Notice that when this "power" is delivered to them, they are then equipped to be witnesses into all the world. *(Acts 1:8)*

Ask For It

I have also noticed that in the Old Testament the anointing was given as God so chose. For instance, David was the choice of God while he was unaware, and busy in the field. But today God has made the Holy Spirit available to all who desire him–that's just it, YOU MUST DESIRE HIM, PRAY TO RECEIVE HIM, ASK AND YE SHALL RECEIVE. If you are not "anointed" of God today, it could be that you have not prayed to receive it. You can be saved and not be anointed! You cannot be anointed and not be saved!

Highly Favored

Throughout the Old Testament, God chose special nations, places, days, years, and people. The relationship between God and man was quite remote. God was thought of as if he were impossible to approach and far away. In Luke 1:28, we see that Mary the Mother of Jesus is one of those who is told by Gabriel that she is "highly favored." Keep in mind that even what is done in the gospels is still the ending of the

Old Testament period. But Jesus brought God down to earth, and Pentecost brought him even closer. As a matter of a fact, He now resides in our hearts.

According to John 15:19, we have been chosen by God, NO ONE IS EXCLUDED! No one is too low, too sinful, or too filthy. Of course, John 3:16 says that God loved the **WORLD** so, that he gave.

What About Me?

Of course, there are those who seem to be blessed beyond others. Are they "highly favored"? Yes. There are those who seem successful in the Kingdom business of the Lord. Are they "anointed"? Yes. But because God is of no respecter of persons, there is nothing that anyone can receive from the Lord that you and I can't get. *(Acts 10:34; James 2:9)* James says you have not because you ask not. *(James 4:2)*

You may be asking, "How do I live under the anointing and be highly favored of the Lord?"

Well, it may be that the difficulty is removed when we understand that the terminology may be different, but all of it really means living obediently while laboring and walking in the spirit and not in the flesh. Ask God to anoint you with the power of the Holy Ghost, and He will. Obey his Word and He will withhold no good thing from you!

Romans 8

I. We Receive the Righteousness of the Law through the Anointing. (v. 4)

A) The Flesh Blocks the Anointing (v. 5)
B) The Anointing Consumes the Mind (v. 5)
C) The Anointing Breaks the Yoke (Isaiah 10:27)

II We Receive Life and Peace Through the Anointing. (v. 6)

A) We have life because He lives in us. (v. 9)

B) We have life because of the resurrection (v. 11)

C) We have life because we mortify the flesh (v. 13)

III. We Receive Sonship through the Anointing. (v. 14)

A) The anointing gives us adoption. (v. 15)

B) The anointing proves our adoption (v. 16)

C) The anointing glorifies our adoption (v. 17)

When your Life is pleasing to the Lord and you pray for His anointing on your life, the oil is symbolic of the Holy Ghost and that covering and filling that He gives. You should know that the anointing not only breaks the yoke or the dominating power of the enemy, but it also makes it difficult for him to get a grip on your soul.

As the oil is a symbol of the Holy Ghost, notice that oil has a way of penetrating things. So although the enemy can't handle us, the Holy Ghost already does!

GOD'S WORD CONCERNING: WHEN PRAISES GO UP!

II Corinthians 10:3-5
Ephesians 6:10-20

Before we begin on this subject, I must say that this is one lesson that cannot be dealt with exhaustively in one hour or even in one week. There is certainly more here than meets the eye, but let us see what we can say to shed some light. Because we know that when praises go up, blessings come down!

No believer will get far if he or she is not aware that we (Christians) are in a war. World War I, World War II, the Civil War, and other wars have all come and gone, but there is one war where that battle is still raging. As a matter of a fact, all other wars, diseases, false concepts, evil ideologies and every thing that is unlike God, is brought on because of this war.

This war is a battle between good and evil, right and wrong, sin and righteousness. We are soldiers in the Lord's army and our battle is spiritual warfare.

The Strategy Is to Tear Down the Strongholds

A stronghold is a geographical place, corporate thought concept, or individual thought concept. The concept of a stronghold comes from the way that an enemy would take charge of some high ground and would build walls, lookout towers, castles, gates, moats, and trenches. Being in a high position with constant watchmen, an enemy could be difficult to conquer. He would see his opposition a long way away and would take whatever countermeasures necessary to defeat his enemy.

An Appropriate Weapon

When battling ignorance, we use the weapon of education. When battling darkness, we use the weapon of light. Medicine is used to defeat sickness. A physical weapon is needed to defeat a physical enemy, but when you come against a spiritual enemy, you need an appropriate weapon! And it must be used in an appropriate way!

Muscle power, arguments, bad tempers, violence, guns, etc., are all-useless against the strongholds of the enemy!

Satan's Army is Organized

Ephesians 6:12 tells us that our battle is not with people, but rather with:

Principalities–Chief Rulers of the Highest Rank in Satan's Army
Powers–2nd to the Chief Rulers
Rulers of Darkness–World Rulers of Darkness
Wickedness in High Places–Wicked Spirits under World Rulers

So, how do we successfully wage war against such a powerful and well-organized enemy?

Through Praise and Worship

II Corinthians 10:5 says we destroy strongholds by:

1) Casting down imaginations.
2) Bringing into captivity every thought.
3) Having a readiness to avenge all disobedience.

Watch Your Mouth!

Have you ever thought about how powerful the mouth is? Do you remember what James, the brother of our Lord, says about the tongue? The mouth has the potential to do both good and evil. *(James 3:3-13)*

Have you ever noticed that whatever you do in life there are always words that go along with the process? Words go with everything, but they come forth from the mouth and the heart. Romans 10:8 says, that the word of faith is already in your mouth. With the mouth, you can talk your way into a blessing or out of a messing!

When Do We Get Guns?

In the comedy "Police Academy," there were all kinds of hilarious misfits, but one that I recall kept asking the question, "Guns, when do we get guns?" Now that you know that we are involved in "spiritual warfare," and that we need an "appropriate weapon," and that those weapons are spiritual, then how do I get mine? Well the truth is you already have what you need.

The Big (Guns) Ammunition!

We have an arsenal that contains **Three Powerful Weapons:**

1) The **Name of Jesus**–Acts 3:6; Matthew 18:19-20; Hebrews 13:15; Acts 4:18 (the enemy knows the power of the Name of Jesus)

2) The **Blood of Jesus**–Romans 5:9; Revelation 12:10-11; Ephesians 1:7

3) The **Word of God**–John 1:1; Romans 10:17; Isaiah 55:11

The "Word" tells us in Revelation 12:11 of the power of the blood and the word.

These are powerful weapons in and of themselves, but there is one problem. They will not activate themselves. You see, these weapons are like a bullet. If I'm not mistaken, a bullet is made up of a shell or casing, with gunpowder on the inside and a lead slug at the other end.

But a bullet is only lethal when placed into a devise that is called a gun that engages a hammer type action that strikes the shell, igniting the gunpowder that fires the slug!

The Big Guns!

So, if the Name, The Blood, and the Word are the ammunition, then preaching, teaching, prayer and praise are the instruments or weapons that we use to defeat the devil.

Something That We Can Do Together!

Preaching, praying, and teaching are done mostly on an individual basis. Praise is something that begins individually, but can be done corporately. Don't forget that where two or three are gathered in the Name of Jesus, we have the promise of his presence.

Psalm 22:3 says, God lives in our praise, he takes up residence in our praise. God does this when one person praises him, so just think of how powerful this can be if we as a body agree with the Word, the Name, and the Blood, and incorporate this into our songs and prayers and into every act of praise and worship.

What Praise Does!

1. Stills the enemy (Psalm 8:1-2)
2. Clothing of the Spirit (Isaiah 61:3)
3. We triumph (Psalm 106:47)

4. Brings revelation (Psalm 49:4)

5. Opens the way for miracles (Psalm 50:23)

6. Bring us into the presence of God (Psalm 100:4)

Now there are two things that God honors:

#1. His Word

#2 Your Faith in His Word.

Therefore, praise, preaching, teaching, and prayer place us in position to not only bring blessings down, but to be victorious in taking this world for Christ.

So, come on, let's go up to the high places and tear the devil's kingdom down!

GOD'S WORD CONCERNING: "THE SIN THAT CAN NOT BE FORGIVEN"

Matthew 12:31-32; Mark 3:28-29
Luke 12:10; Hebrews 6:4, 10:26

What is Sin? The Word of God says that sin is the transgression of the Law of God. *(I John 3:4)*

Sin (**Greek word Harmartia**)–Missing the mark, always in a moral sense, a sin whether by commission or by omission in thought, word, or in deed.

Presumptuous Sin

Presumptuous Sin is one committed willfully, knowingly, and openly in defiance of the law; a sin of ignorance is an act of breaking the law without knowing that the law is being violated. (Numbers 15:30-31)

Unpardonable Sin

What about the **Unpardonable Sin**? For many years, people were taught that cursing God and suicide were the unpardonable sins. But is that the truth? Most people thought that suicide was the "unpardonable sin" because of the idea that you can hardly ask forgiveness for such a thing once you have just taken your own life. But even this theory suggests other things, such as each individual sin that we commit throws us out of the hand of the Lord. And we know, that this cannot be so because the forgiveness of Christ covers the believer's **past, present, and future,** although there may be some loss of victorious joy and reward in the life to come. And furthermore, our idea of cursing God in America is weak. Although I don't encourage you to take the name of the Lord in vain in profane language, "cursing" God is much more than what we think.

More on Suicide

Knowing that the first law of life is said to be the law of self-preservation, when a person takes his own life, in many cases, their mental health must be at an all-time low. They are usually victims of deep depression and other imbalances that cause a self-destructive behavior. God will judge them based upon their mental health also. If you recall the ad man in the cemetery had demonic forces within driving him to destroy himself. Jesus rebuked them, not him. *(Mark 5)*

Mercy and grace were available to those who commit sins of ignorance. There can be no sin or penalty for sin if there is no law clearly stated. *(Romans 4:15)*

Something Must Be Done

Because God is a Holy God, he cannot tolerate sin. Sin must be dealt with, and the only way that God deals with sin is by death. Sin is so serious that God, with all of his power, cannot wink at sin. He can't ignore it, forget it, or rationalize it. God must require that the soul that sinneth must die! *(Ezekiel 18:4)* The wages of sin is death, but the gift of God is eternal life through Christ Jesus our Lord. *(Romans 6:23)*

The Beauty of Forgiveness

Now let us explore what it means to forgive. To forgive means to take responsibility for the charges of another. It means to free one from a moral obligation to correct something that one has done wrong.

Let us look at an example: If a man kills another man, then the law of God says that the murderer is worthy of death. Keep in mind the things that happen when this kind of crime takes place. Maybe, he was married; maybe there were children. Now, there is a wife who has no husband and children who have no father. There is also the trauma, the pain and the pressure that family will have to endure for many years to come.

For them to now say, "I forgive you" (though others may still prosecute), that family is saying "you don't have to pay for what you've done, we will bear the expense!"

Most of us would not even consider doing this, and understand me here: I'm not trying to persuade you on this issue either way. But I must say that this is what God has done for us.

What I am saying is this: we need to understand how serious sin really is. The above illustration should help us to see that sin is really terrible! We deserve death, and God says, "I'll bear the expense!"

But how did He bear the expense? By just writing it off? No! A Holy God couldn't do that! God bore the expense by dying in our place. That's how wonderful God is!

> **I John 1:9** tells us that if we confess our sins God will forgive us.
>
> **II Chronicles 7:14** says if we would return to God, God will forgive us of our sins.
>
> **Isaiah 1:18** say no matter how bad our sins may be, he wants to wash us completely.

But as willing as God is in forgiving our sin, there is a sin that God will not forgive. Even God has a limit to his forgiveness!

That Brings Us to Blasphemy

Blasphemy is the act of insulting, cursing, or in regards to the Holy Spirit, giving credit to Satan for what the Holy Ghost has done.

Some Examples of Blasphemy:

Speak Evil of	(Jude 8; Ephesians 4:31
Rail	(I Timothy 6:4; II Peter 2:11)
Revile	(Matthew 27:39)
Defame	(I Corinthians 4:13)
Slander	(Romans 3:8)
Insult by Blasphemy	(Matthew 12:31)

It seems that Hebrew 6:4-5 brings more light to the subject. Mind you, we are not simply talking about someone saying something just from the mouth. You see, that which is uttered from the mouth is born in the heart. *(Romans 10:10)*

The blasphemer is one who has gone beyond the sin of ignorance (when one does something that he doesn't realize is wrong). He is arrogant so much so concerning his disbelief in God that he has the audacity to speak it. At least the "fool" has said in his heart, "there is no God." *(Psalm 14:1, 53:1).* But the blasphemer actually speaks it! He speaks it because it is in his heart. Now for this to occupy his heart then this person has obviously gone into a state that we recently talked about called "apostasy."

The **"Apostate"** has been a **Believer,** but drifted into a **Backslidden** position and rather than to repent, he has fallen all the way down into **Total Rejection of God**.

Hebrews tell us that once one has been **Enlightened** and has **Tasted** and has been a **Partaker** (all past tense), if one falls away (apostatize) he cannot return! Now, I don't think that salvation is impossible for them because of God having any inability, but they can't be revived at this point because of their own hardened heart.

Finally, Hebrews 10:26 says that once we cross the line into a cold, callous attitude toward the work of the Holy Ghost, who is in operation in this dispensation, then we become apostate in our relationship and blasphemous in our conversation. Never having repented and having become so hardened by sin, we at this point refuse to repent, and in death there is no way that salvation is possible!

Daily, we should pray for the Lord to keep his hand upon us, that we stay close to him, guided by his light, secured by his arm, and warmed by his love, so that we never lose the taste of God in our lives.

GOD'S WORD CONCERNING: "VERY SUPERSTITIOUS"

When you believe in things that you don't understand, then you suffer...superstition ain't the way!
Stevie Wonder

Just to name a Few!

• Don't split the pole	Bad Luck
• Don't put your purse on the floor	Broke For Life
• Never let a black cat cross your path	Bad Luck
• Don't break a mirror	Bad Luck
• Don't sweep my feet	Bad Luck

- A man should never throw a hat on the bed–causes a woman to bear
- If you dream about fish that means that someone is going to have a baby
- Fix black-eyed peas on New Years Day
- Never walk under a ladder
- Different things will follow throughout the year based on whether a man or a woman walks into the house first on New Years Day
- If your nose itches, somebody's coming
- If your hand itches, expect some money
- Step on a crack; break your mother's back.
- Never open an umbrella in the house
- If you're talking to one person and you call that person by a third person's name, it is assumed that the third person is talking about you
- Walking around with only one shoe will cause you to lose the one you love

- When a dog howls that means someone will die!
- No 13th Floor in most hotels
- Friday the 13th
- Don't let more than one person do your hair at the same time
- Spit on a broom if you have had bad luck

Are there more?

____
____
____
____
____
____

Superstitious comes from the Geek word *Deisidaimonia,* "to reverence the god," also to be devout without the knowledge of God.

The Word of God deals with those who had a version of godliness, that really had no power! *(II Timothy 3:5-7) (Acts 17:16-22)*

After leaving its Philippi and other towns that rejected the Gospel of Christ, Paul went to Athens. It was there that he would wait for the rest of his evangelistic team to meet up with him. But while waiting for them, Paul saw that there was much work to be done right there where he was. Paul had high hopes of doing a great work in Athens. Winning this city for Christ would mean a great deal to the Kingdom of Christ.

Athens was known for its intellectuals, philosophers, and Greek mythology. Their schools of grammar, rhetoric, dialectics, and philosophy were always crowded.

Some of the gods that they believed in were Mercury, the god of eloquence; and Diana, the goddess of light by night, also known as the Protectress of Youth, especially to those of her same sex. She was also believed to assist in the birthing of children. Jupiter controlled the weather, decided which battles should be fought, which victories would be won, and also gave them wine.

After looking around for a while, Paul noticed that this city had so many different gods, that most of their time was spent in telling or hearing some new thing. *(Acts 17:16, 21)*

Here's the Trick!

#1. The trick of the devil was to flood this sophisticated, intellectual city with so much idolatry and superstition that when the Gospel of Christ would be introduced, it would be looked at as just another philosophy or superstition. Nothing more. Nothing less.

#2. Also, it was against the law in Athens to introduce a new god. Can you believe that? They had so many gods that this gave reason to pass legislation that would allow everything in but Christ. (Truth!) Legally, they could say, "We have enough gods!"

This is what superstition does: It attempts to lessen the power of the Gospel by having people frightened by other rules, cautions and customs of other deities. *(Acts 17:25)*

It also blocks the truth of Christ, because we are not able to have total trust in Christ while remaining in bondage to superstition. *(Acts 17:28-29)*

It is my belief that much of what we call superstition probably just makes good sense, but has no real power to determine the destiny of our lives. For instance, it's just good sense to avoid walking under a ladder, something may fall on your head. You should avoid breaking a mirror. You could get cut. You shouldn't open an umbrella in the house, something could get broken. And as far as that hat on the bed, I think you had better concern yourself with that an on the bed. If his hat is on your bed, you are already in trouble. What is he doing in your bedroom?

As far as a black cat crossing my path, that is bad luck for the cat, if I'm driving my car. When two people are walking together and one splits a pole, symbolically, it just doesn't look right. You're supposed to be together. And with the kind of things that we encounter with a broom, it's just not good to sweep that same dirt onto your shoes or feet. It's just not clean.

I must admit that much of the rest just makes no sense and needs to be considered useless tricks of the devil to keep Christians and unbelievers fearful instead of bold in the Gospel of Christ.

Christian Must Know Some Things!

> No weapon formed against us shall prosper!
> *(Isaiah 54:17)*
> We have not been given the spirit of fear!
> *(II Timothy 1:7-8)*
> We are to avoid vain, useless talking!
> *(I Timothy 6:20; II Timothy 2:16)*
> We are no longer in darkness!
> *(Ephesians 5:8)*
> Every thing we do now is unto the Lord!
> *(I Corinthians 10:31)*

We are not to give heed to worldly rules saying touch not, taste not. Hear what Colossians 2:20-23 has to say:

> *Since you died with Christ to the basic principles of this world, why, as though you still belonged to it, do you submit to its rules? "Do not handle! Do not taste! Do not touch!" These are all destined to perish with use, because they are based on human commands and teach-*

ings. Such regulations indeed have an appearance of wisdom, with their self-imposed worship, their false humility and their harsh treatment of the body, but they lack any value in restraining sensual indulgence.[7]

GOD'S WORD CONCERNING: FOR THE LOVE OF MONEY!

I Timothy 6:1-21
Hebrews 13:5

"A woman will sell her precious body. People can't even walk the street because of some piece of paper that carries a lot of weight. For the love of money is the root of all evil, and it does funny things to some people. Give me a nickel, brother, can you spare a dime. Money can drive some people out of their mind!"
The O'Jays

Francs, Pesos, Denarius, Yen, Drachmas, Dollars, Bread, Green, Ends, and even Duckies

When you think about it, money is a powerful thing. If you have it, you can do so many things. With enough money, you can live wherever you want to live, wear whatever you want to wear, eat whatever you want to eat, drive whatever you want to drive, and do whatever you want to do. Financial freedom sounds like music to our ears.

I mean, imagine all your bills being paid. **I MEAN PAID!** Your house is paid off; you have enough savings for retirement; you can vacation anywhere you chose, and stay for more than a couple of days or weeks. There are so many things that you can do when you have money.

Now on the other hand, when you don't have money, there are times when it seems that the world is crashing down all around you. If allowed to do so, money can destroy a country, a state, a city, a church, a family, and even a marriage. And I don't simply mean having no money, but having it can be dangerous also!

You see, money is a tool. It has no character, priorities, personality, or goals. It has no principles or morals. It simply depends on the values of the one who possesses it. That's why "money" is not the root of all evil, it's the "**Love**" of it that is.

Money, like many things in this world, is a good slave but a poor master. As long as you remain in charge of it, then it can work for you. But when money becomes your master, you would surprise yourself by the things that you just might do to get your hands on it.

When Money Has Become Your Master, You Will:

- Have co-workers to punch you in or out while absent.
- Cheat on insurance claims.
- Cheat on income tax.
- Cheat on tithe to the Lord.
- Receive assistance though you are able to work.
- Engage in lotteries, riverboats, gambling and pyramids.
- Get rich quick schemes.
- Lawsuits for profit.

And the list goes on and on and on.

In order to live a life that truly gives glory to the Lord, one needs to know the difference between desiring to live comfortably and loving money. And the difference between being satisfied and content. (Hebrews 13:5, Philippians 4:11)

Check Yourself for Financial Bondage

(According to Larry Burkett)

Overdue Bills	(Proverbs 27:12)
Investment Worries	(Matthew 6:24-25)
Get Rich Quick Attitude	(Proverbs 28:20)
No Gainful Employment	(II Thessalonians 3:10)

Deceitfulness	(Luke 16:10)
Greediness	(Ephesians 5:5)
Covetousness	
Family Need Unmet	(I Timothy 5:8)
Unmet Christian Needs	(James 2:15-16)
Over-commitment to Work	
Money Entanglements	
Financial Unfairness	(Proverbs 28:8)
Lack of Commitment to God's Work	(Proverbs 3:9-10)
Financial Superiority	
Financial Resentment	(John 6:27)

Look at These:

Rich Through Christ–Wicked Refuse to Repay
(II Corinthians 9:11, Proverbs 30:8-9, Psalm 37:21)

Credit Makes Slaves–Pleasure Seekers–Basic Principle
Proverbs 22:7, Proverbs 21:17, Luke 16:10

The Will of God in our lives concerning money ought to be to prepare ourselves educationally to gain the type of employment that will allow us to (1) glorify God, (2) earn an honest living, and (3) discover the self-fulfillment that we desire by helping others on the road of life.

It is also the will of God that we learn to live within our own means. Covetousness leads to impulsive purchases, keeping up with the Joneses, anxiety, and resentment. Paul says that regardless of my state, I have learned to be content. *(Philippians 4:11)*

I Our Attitude Toward Those Who Have Money (vs. 1-8)

A) Respect the unbeliever to avoid blasphemy. (v. 1)
B) Respect the Believer because he is a Brother (v. 2)
C) Recognize true gain (vs. 3-8)

II Our Attitude Toward Money (vs. 9-16)

A) The desire for riches (v. 9)
B) The love for riches (v. 10)
C) The pursuit for riches (v. 11-16)

III The Attitude of the Rich Toward Others (vs. 17-21)

A) All are equal (v. 17)
B) Use money to bless others (v. 18)
C) Save toward the Kingdom (vs. 19-21)

GOD'S WORD CONCERNING: HOW CAN I EVER FORGIVE?

Luke 22:34

Everywhere that we turn, there are wounded souls. People today seem to have all sorts of motives for hurting one another. People will hurt you for money, sex, power, fun, or just to pass the time away. And by now you should know that people don't have to have an understandable reason for what they do.

There are folks that don't like you and they don't have a reason. They just don't like you. You haven't said the wrong thing or done the wrong thing to them. They just don't like you!

Whatever the case, now you've been wounded. And in many cases, by someone you love and you know... believe... think... thought that they loved you. Maybe you shared your deepest secrets, places, times, dates, details, and before you knew it, all your business was scattered all over town.

The Question:

For a while, your constant question is: **WHAT?** Then your next question that continues on for another while is: **WHY?**

After this has happened to you a few times, it doesn't take long to lose faith in people. I mean you become afraid that just about everybody has a hidden agenda. Even the most sincere become suspect. Even the most faithful become frightening. Even the most honorable seem to have some harmful hope of you becoming their next victim.

All of us have been there. We all know too well that this is not a good place to be. The hurt, the pain, and the anguish. It's almost more than one can bear. I hear you saying, "What do I do?" **Forgive?** Then there are those same two questions again: you say, "Which ones?" Oh yes, **WHAT? And then WHY?**

Because you are a child of God, you are Christlike. You have never been instructed to trust in men. Psalm 71 says, "*In thee oh Lord do I put my trust.*"

<u>So Now You Want to Know</u>

"How Can I Ever Forgive?"

Well, though it may not be simple, in your heart you and I both know that it's right. It's right because Jesus said it, Jesus did it, and in your spirit you know it!

Who among us can boast of being more misused and abused than Christ? He was falsely accused, misunderstood, beaten, rebuked, betrayed, denied, forsook, hated, scorned, talked about. And yet he trusted in the Father enough to say, "Father, forgive them for they know not what they do!"

Sure, they knew on the surface what they were doing when they nailed his hands. Sure, they knew on the surface what they were doing when the riveted his feet. But Jesus possessed a higher thinking capacity than his offenders. *(Philippians 2:5-11)*

He **Knew** some things that they didn't know. And so must you. You must know **Who** you are and **Whose** you are, and also you must Know **Why** you are.

1) I am_________________.

2) I am a Child of God.

3) I am Here to Glorify God.

Nothing can ever **interfere** with that. Nothing can ever **overshadow** that. Nothing can ever **cancel** that. Therefore, I must respond and react to every situation of life with these things in mind. Again, it's not easy, but it's right.

Let's look at this issue of **Forgive and Forget.**

You may remember this definition from our lesson on "The Sin That Cannot Be Forgiven."

The Beauty of Forgiveness

Let us explore what it means to **Forgive**. To forgive means to take responsibility for the charges of another. It means to free one from a moral obligation to correct something that one has done wrong.

Because one forgives doesn't give us some special sixth sense of selective amnesia. Forgetting does not in this case mean that there is no remembrance of the offense. It simply means that once it has been dealt with, you move on with your life! YOUR LIFE – you remember –YOU HAVE A LIFE! You must press on!

Even this doesn't mean that you place yourself in position to repeat the same offense, it only means stay on course and let nothing sway you from that which **YOU KNOW**!

So many along life's highway have wrecked and been pulled over to the shoulder and been abandoned. But you can't allow this. You have got to drive on.

You've got to have a Song

Here's one for you: "*Onward Christian soldier marching as to war with the cross of Jesus going on before. Christ the royal master leads against the foe. Onward into battle, see his banners go.*"

"While living the crucified life, keep looking unto the Father, as Jesus did, for direction, relation, and completion. He will give you the power to forgive."

Direction Father Forgive
Relation Why Hast Thou Forsaken Me?
Completion Into Thy Hands I Commend My Spirit.

GOD'S WORD CONCERNING: HOW DO YOU <u>KNOW</u> THAT YOU'RE SAVED?

The first question that needs to be asked is, "What is Salvation?" Salvation is simply knowing God; to be in relationship with God through Jesus Christ. *(John 17:3)* Of course, as a result of knowing God, there are other things that come into play. Such as forgiveness, power, the promises of God and more. But to know Him is first.

Most of the time when this subject is dealt with, people immediately think in terms of where we are going when Christ returns. They begin to envision streets of gold, the homeland of the soul, trees with fruit and leaves that are good for the healing of the nation, gates of pearl, and throne rooms of crystal.

Yes, we can't help but think of a place where the present disturbances will reign no more. As a matter of fact, where we are going is a land of "No More." No more setbacks, setups, set outs, or backsets. Yes, a time when everyday will be Sunday and the Sabbath will have no end. Every month will be the month of May, and every year the year of Jubilee. Nothing but "Howdy, Howdy," and never "Good–Bye."
But before you simply prepare yourself for tomorrow you need something to hold you today! Not only that, you also need assurance that your yesterday has been properly dealt with. The Good News (*the Gospel*) is that Salvation has as much to do with your yesterday and today as it does your tomorrow. Jesus says the difference is made just by <u>KNOWING GOD!</u>

<u>Let's Look at Yesterday</u>

Before we met the Lord, we were what the Bible calls lost, sinners, wicked, children of wrath, and ungodly. Even if you were not a bad person, even if you just didn't know any better, you were lost, not because you were so devilish, but simply because you DIDN'T KNOW GOD!

But even when you didn't know him, he knew you. (*Jeremiah 1:5)* And had chosen you before the foundation of the world. (*Ephesians 1:4)* And has brought you close to him by the Blood of Jesus. (*Ephesians. 2:13)*

But it's even more exciting to know that God was doing all of this while you and I were yet sinners. (*Romans 5:6-8)*

<u>Let us Look at our Tomorrow</u>

Earlier, we talked about the expectations that are sure to take place and here we shall go a little further.

The Apostle Paul and Peter both speak of crowns that are reserved for those who trust in the Lord. (*II Timothy 4:8, I Peter 5:4, 6)* The writer of the Book of Hebrews clearly stated that there is yet a "rest" coming that we have not yet experienced and we are to labor here until we enter it. (*Hebrews 4:9-11)* Like Abraham, we yearn for a different city: one with zero pollution, zero crime, zero unemployment. A city built by God. (*Hebrews 11:10)*

<u>What About Today</u>

Now if you are going to **KNOW** that you are saved, this knowledge will not come from any emotional or dramatic experience. All of these are good but at their best, weak! Feelings are unreliable. They can't be trusted. What we need is facts, especially with something this important. Understand me when I say that there is nothing wrong with feeling the spirit, running, shouting, and screaming if you feel like it, but when you get through with the physical, you better know something that is **spiritual and factual**.

Let me ask you this: If you are going to base your salvation on a feeling that you get, then what do you do when you just don't feel like it? All of us have days when we don't feel like it. But that's when we rest on the facts.

That means you must, first of all, totally believe that the Word of God is the "**Word of God**." In a sense, the rest is relatively easy. Just think what your life would be like if you would truly say, "God Said It, I Believe It, That Settles It." Concerning our mansion Jesus said, "If it were not so, I would have told you!" *(John 14:2)* You should underline every promise of God in your heart with that.

Finally, I KNOW I'm Saved

I know I'm saved because I qualify as WHOSOEVER.
(John 3:16)
I know I'm saved because there is love in my heart
(I John 3:14)
I know I'm saved because I believe God's Word
(I John 5:11-12)

"I know I've been changed, the angels in Heaven done signed my name..."

GOD'S WORD CONCERNING: THE MINISTRY OF ANGELS Part I

The term "angels" seems to describe all of heaven's inhabitants outside of the redeemed. With this in mind, we are also aware that "angels" are not all the same because they are made up of Cherubim, Seraphim, Principalities, and Powers.

Part One of this Lesson will deal with these facts:

I. They are Immortal Spirits

II. They Possess Great Knowledge

III. They are Very Active and Powerful

IV. They are Sinless and Obedient

Part Two of this Lesson will deal with:

I. Their Presence at the Beginning of Sainthood

II. Their Watchfulness and Guardian Work Concerning the Steps of Saints

III. Their conveyance of the Souls of the Dead in Christ to Heaven

IV. Their service to Us (the heirs of Salvation) When Christ Returns

This lesson only deals with those angels who have remained faithful to the Lord.

Now before we go into the area of the angels themselves, let us look at the teachings of:

Theophanies

While there are many appearances of angels (Dr. Dake's sites some 104 appearances) throughout the Scriptures, there are some that were said to be angelic, by our predecessors, which were not angels at all.

For example, the "voice" that came to Adam after he had sinned was actually Christ himself. *(Genesis 3:8)* The entourage that came to Abraham to discuss the birth of Isaac and the destruction of Sodom and Gomorrah was led by Christ. *(Genesis 18)* When Joshua was in need of guidance, the captain of the Lord of Host that came to him was Christ. *(Joshua 5:14)* I think that it ought to be said here that we know this to be the Lord Jesus because worship was both required and allowed. *(See v. 15)*

There are many more theophanies that time and space will not allow us to discuss, but rest assured that Jesus is truly God and was before the foundation of the world. It's exciting to know that he made appearances in both the Old and the New Testaments.

Angels are Immortal Spirits

Because of the fact that angels are spirits, they have the ability to possess three important things: Thought, will, and reflection. Yet, they are in general contrast with matter, for they are body-less. Jesus proved this when he said to the disciples, handle me, and see; for a spirit hath not flesh and bones, as you see me have. *(Luke 24:39)*

Luke 20:36 tells us that the angels are immortal by the will of God. Part of the reason why they are immortal is because God requires everlasting praise and worship. And furthermore, they are on an eternal research project as they study the incomprehensible love of God.

Angels are Filled with Knowledge

Although angels possess great knowledge, it goes without saying that they are not omniscient. Only God is. Not even Satan knows all that

God knows, for even he, as powerful as he is, is no more than a mighty but **fallen** angel.

Angels are Powerful

Many times in Scripture we find Biblical writers attempting to convey ideas that were difficult to translate with our finite minds and language. Angels having wings is one of those difficult concepts. Wings belonging to angels are to be understood as simply the only human expression available to describe such swift and powerful movement as exhibited by these spiritual beings. But to take this literally would be a mistake, after all, the fastest flying being in this world moves at a snail's speed compared to the swiftness of an angel.

Psalm 53:20 says that angels "excel in strength." Again, their strength as with their knowledge, is not unlimited but simply dependent upon God. Just to give you an idea of the power of angels, II Kings 19:35 and Isaiah 37:36 tell us that in one night, one angel destroyed 185,000 men. It's easy to see why II Thessalonians 1:7 says that the second coming of Christ will be ushered in by his Mighty Angels.

Angel are Sinless and Obedient

God made man a little lower than the angels. *(Psalm 8:5)* With this in mind, the purity of the angels is obviously on an altogether different level than man. Matthew 25:31 refers to them as "Holy Angels."

Jesus teaches **US** to pray in Matthew 6:13-19. In that prayer we are to understand that the will of God is perfectly done in heaven without contradiction. The only interest of the Holy Angels of God is to do the will of God. They have no other agenda. No other schedule. No other concerns. It has been said that if one angel was sent to oversee a nation and another to watch over a baby, neither would be jealous or envious of the task of the other, for the only concern of angels is to do the will of God.
As we study the work of these immortal spirits who are in possession

of great knowledge, power and activity, and who have remained faithful, sinless and obedient to God, I believe we will develop a wonderful appreciation for our wondrous God and His glorious ways.

GOD'S WORD CONCERNING: THE MINISTRY OF ANGELS PART II

Before we go into the second part of our lesson, allow me to address some of the questions that were raised in a lesson concerning cherubim and seraphim.

The Society of Angels in the spirit realm seems to be made up of four different levels. They are as follows: cherubim, seraphim, principalities, and powers. Cherubim and seraphim are those who have remained faithful to God and have not fallen into sin. Those known as principalities and powers are under the rule of Satan. Their rank or authority seems to be seen in the above order. Cherubim are higher in authority than seraphim. Principalities are higher in rank than that of powers.

The proper singular usage for cherubim is cherub and the proper singular usage for seraphim is seraph. Notwithstanding, there are places in the Scripture where the word cherubim and seraphim are also seen. In the first chapter of Ezekiel, we see that cherubim have four faces, four wings and four hands. They have characteristics of animals as well as man. The four faces consist of the face of a man, a lion, an ox, and an eagle. They fly with the speed of lightning and with the sound of thunder. Their only will is to do the will of the Lord.

Cherubim are involved at some level with the holiness of God as violated by sin. They vindicate the righteousness of God. *(Exodus 25:17-20)* In Ezekiel, we also see them upholding the Throne of God.

This may be particularly interesting: When man sinned, God placed cherubim around the Tree of Life to keep the way of the tree. It has been said that the reason was to keep man from the tree. After all, if man, in his sinful state, had eaten of the tree, he would forever live. How terrible that would be! So, why did God place cherubim around the Tree of Life? Let's go a little deeper. It's not that God doesn't want us to come to the Tree; He just wants us to come the right way. When Adam and Eve were evicted from the garden, the Cherubim were there to remind them that the only way back was through the sacrifice that they had experienced when God killed some type of animal and made them skins. In order to do this, Adam and Eve had to have come under the Blood that was representative of the death, burial and resurrection of Jesus Christ. They could return, but only by way of the Blood.

Willmington says that their duties were to:

> Guard and to vindicate the righteousness of God.
> *(Exodus 26:1; 36:8, 35)*
>
> To aid in the administration of the government of God.
> *(I Samuel 4:4; Psalms 80:1, 99:1; Ezekiel 1:22-26)*

To be eternal reminders of the blessed earthly ministry of the Lord Jesus Christ. This is seen in the faces of the cherubim:

Matthew	Jews	King	Lion
Mark	Romans	Servant	Ox
Luke	Greeks	Human	Man
John	Universe	God	Eagle

The Seraphim were a little different in appearance. Isaiah saw them in the Temple when he saw the Lord. They had six wings: two that they used to cover their faces in humility; two more that they used to cover their feet in respect; and another set of two that they used to fly away. Not much is disclosed about the appearance of their faces, hands and feet because of their behavior above. Though we do gather that they had faces, hands, feet, and voices, Isaiah says he saw one of their hands because one took a coal from the altar and purged his sins with it to prepare him for service in the work of the Lord. I would also like to add that Isaiah observed these heavenly beings occupied in (1) the celebration of the praise of God concerning his holiness and power, and (2) the act of serving as a medium of communication between heaven and earth.

Seraphim have something to do with the uncleanness of the people of God. They are beings expressive of the Divine holiness of God and demand that saints shall be cleansed before they can serve.

You should also be aware of the fact that the spirit realm is as real and diverse as the physical. Just as with earth, heaven is a place (a real place) where God, the angels (cherubim and seraphim), other spiritual beings, and the redeemed live. Heaven has walls, streets, gates, trees, rivers, specific places, and a palace, which is the Throne of God! *(Revelation 21:1-2; 10-27; 22:1-3)*

Revelation 19:11 even speaks of heavenly horses. Read the 14th verse. I think this will help us to develop a better understanding. The Bible says that the things that are seen are temporary, but the things that are unseen are eternal. We must understand that the physical world was not here first. The spiritual world was the original pattern that God used to create the physical world. *(I Corinthians 2:9-10, II Corinthians 4:18)*

Therefore, whatever we have in this world, these things and more are already in heaven. Only in heaven they are not mingled with the negatives that we have in this sinful world.

Now let us look at Part II.

<u>Angels are Involved With Us at the Beginning of Sainthood</u>

Luke 15:10 tells us that the angels have such a great understanding concerning spiritual things that while many of us are unconcerned about the souls of the lost, angels rejoice when a sinner comes to Christ. They understand that this is a soul that will not be going to hell. This soul now will live eternally with Christ in peace and joy. Because the angels are spiritually mature, they understand and they shout!

Angels Watch and Guard the Steps of the Saints

Psalm 91:10-12 teaches us that God is so concerned about the welfare of his saints that he has commanded them to take special care of us. "Lest thou dash thy foot against a stone." God doesn't want you to even hurt your smallest toe! But Matthew 18:10 takes it even a little deeper; he says that it is dangerous to tamper with his saints. We can rejoice because God has angels constantly reporting to him concerning our condition. The text says that they are "always" beholding God's face. Imagine that. Angels are continually getting in God's face about you and I. The wondrous word here is that Jesus called them "their angels." They belong to us to guard and keep us. Hallelujah.

Angels Carry the Dead in Christ to Heaven

Luke 16:22 teaches us that this man Lazarus who had been sick, despised, and neglected in this world, died. Though his life had been rough and harsh, when he died, his journey to heaven was by way of a heavenly entourage. The rich man died and immediately went to hell with no escort, no entourage. But the Bible says that Lazarus was carried by the angels! One glad morning when this life is over, with the help of the angels and the power of God, I'll fly away!

Angels will continue to Serve us when Christ Returns

Matthew 24:31 says that when Christ returns, it's going to be some kind of gathering. A trumpet will sound; the angels will disburse to every direction of the compass. Their business will be to gather up every soul, red, yellow, black, brown, and white. Yes, they shall gather up the rich, the poor, the educated and the illiterate, the good, the bad and, the ugly who have received Christ as their personal savior. What a meeting that's going to be! When we all get to heaven, what a day of rejoicing that will be. When we all see Jesus, we'll sing and shout the victory.

It's exciting to think of how great a reunion this is going to be. Not only will we be reunited with parents, family, friends and loved ones, but we will have the chance to meet the Old and New Testament saints that we have learned so much from. But there's more; when we get to heaven, we will finally have the chance to meet the angels who have been watching over us all night and all day!

"But when I see Jesus...Amen!"

GOD'S WORD CONCERNING: THE FALL OF LUCIFER

This study of angelology is an intriguing one. To come to the understanding that heaven is a real place, with real places, people and things, is a total eye-opening experience. There are streets, buildings, agriculture, light, water: as a matter of a fact, everything that we have on earth is in heaven, and more. The Scriptures say that "eyes have not seen, ears have not heard, and hearts have not received the good things that are in store in heaven for those that love the Lord. *(I Corinthians 2:9)*

But as we study the Ministry of Angels, our work would be incomplete if we didn't take at least a brief look at "The Fall of Lucifer." As we look at this study, let us pay close attention to his mistakes, that we not be responsible for repeating them. Jesus said that He beheld Satan as lightning fall from heaven. *(Luke 10:18)*

The Anointed Cherub That Covereth

In many places in the Word of God, there are passages that have deeper meanings and even double meanings, beyond what is clearly seen on the surface. The Garden of Eden dialogue is a good example. When God cursed the serpent, he not only cursed it, but also Satan. When he pronounced judgment upon Eve, He also included all of womankind. And in the case of Adam, all mankind was included in having to wrestle with the ground and to water it with his sweat in order to eat. Ezekiel 28:1-10 follows a similar pattern. According to Josephus, a non-biblical Jewish historian, the King of Tyre was an actual person who really went through what is recorded in verses 1-10. But by verse 11, the focus moves over to this one who was in the "Garden of Eden." One who sealed up the sum, was perfect in wisdom, and perfect in beauty.

As we look at verse 13-15, it seems to elaborate on the three ideas presented in verse 12.

Lucifer the Most Beautiful

That Lucifer was in Eden, the Garden of God, suggests that this cannot be a mere human king. Before God created man, Lucifer was in the Garden. Not only present, but the dominant one in all of his ways.

To see him was to see every color of the rainbow. He was covered with sardis, topaz, diamond, beryl, onyx, jasper, sapphire, emerald, carbuncle, and gold. Not only was he beautiful standing idle, but he was also music when in motion. When God created him, he placed pipes within that were the source of lovely music to the glory of God. Keep in mind that when the cherubim of Ezekiel 1:10 moved, it was like the sound of thunder and the sight of lightning. To combine this with the beauty and music of Lucifer must have been a magnificent audio and video experience.

Lucifer the Most Powerful

We have already discovered that cherubim are the protectors of the Throne of God. They uphold the throne and all that has to do with the Majesty of God. Lucifer was more than a cherub. He was the "Anointed Cherub That Covereth."

He was over all things and under only God. When I say "God," it is to be understood that God the Father, Son and Holy Ghost is meant. Keep in mind that Jesus is God in human form. But in a sense, Lucifer actually had to have become jealous of Jesus, whom God has given a Name that is above every Name. All of the honor and glory that he had was not enough. He lost touch with the fact that, what he was God made him, and what he had God gave him, and where he was God placed him. God says in verse 14b "I have set thee so!"

While he was yet in heaven and in right relationship with God, he was trusted with power and authority to walk among the stones of fire, which may suggest that all other angels were simply little glimmering, flickering lamps compared to the glorious brightness and power of Lucifer.

Lucifer the Most Dutiful

It's hard to imagine one so diabolical, one so evil as Satan, having been the most perfect in all his ways. Don't just believe me, God's Word says that he was perfect in all of his behavior, until iniquity was found in him.

For the Word to say "iniquity" was found, implies that it was hidden. Have you noticed that "sin" can only be hidden for a while, but eventually it will surface? Lucifer's sin was probably hidden from other angels, but God found it.

As we look closely at verses 16-18, it becomes clear that the fall of Lucifer came as a result of him becoming intoxicated with his own self-worth.

Look at what it says:

1) The Multitude of Thy Merchandise
2) Because of Thy Beauty
3) The Multitude of Thy Iniquities.

Pride, then, is the cause of the fall of Lucifer. And the sad truth is that so many have followed his pitiful example. We should always remember what the Book of Proverbs says in Chapter 16:18: "*Pride goeth before destruction and a haughty spirit before a fall.*"

For more information on the fall of Lucifer, look at Isaiah 14:12-15.

GOD'S WORD CONCERNING: THE PRESENT WORK OF SATAN

I Peter 5:8

In our previous lesson, we looked at the fall of Lucifer. In that lesson, we attempted to uncover how Satan, then known as Lucifer, the "Anointed Cherub that Covereth," fell from the level of holiness, purity, and wisdom that he once had. He was perfect in knowledge, beauty, and behavior. God had entrusted him with power and authority, and he even looked good while executing his office.

You know, there is a lot that we can learn from everybody. Don't ever say that you can't learn anything from this one, or that one. Many of you have seen the television commercial that is more of an infomercial about seatbelt safety. There are two "experimental dummies" in the picture that say "wear your seatbelts, because you can learn a lot from a dummy." Many of us think that we can only learn from "smart" people, but the stupidity of Satan has taught many a lesson. You see, we learn how to do right from those who do right, and we learn how not to do wrong from people who do wrong. Oh, my brothers and sisters, please don't make the mistakes that Satan has made.

Isn't it sad to hear the words of Isaiah 14:12: "How art thou fallen from heaven, O Lucifer, son of the morning! How art thou cut down to the ground, which didst weaken the nations?" Now this verse not only reveals his crimes, but it also shows us that what he was guilty of began before Adam was created. And his diabolical work continues even unto this present moment.

<u>Satan is Presently in Charge of this World</u>

One battle that seems to be ongoing is the task of getting people to see that the devil is not in hell, he doesn't wear a red suit, nor does he have horns or a pitchfork in hand. As a matter of a fact, you might be surprised to know that the enemy doesn't appear to be the "enemy." II Corinthians 11:14 says, "And no marvel; for Satan himself is transformed into an angel of light." This means that Satan is a master at disguises. You may be deceived easily if you are looking for him to approach you one way and he shows up another. Keep in mind that just because he was thrown out of heaven doesn't mean that he lost the beauty and knowledge that he had in heaven. He probably looks the same as he once did. Only now he no longer has the glory of God upon him.

Even in this world, a person's appearance doesn't change immediately when they turn to a life of crime. As a matter of a fact, some of them are some of the most beautiful folks to look at. They have money, clothes, jewelry, cars, friends, good jobs and beautiful people love to be around them. Oh yes, if you didn't know better you would think that they must be doing all right by God, based on how blessed they appear to be.

But the Bible calls Satan "the Prince of the power of the air, the spirit that now worketh in the children of disobedience." *(Ephesians 2:2)* This world doesn't belong to Christ. This world doesn't love Christ, nor does it exalt, or obey Christ. This is Satan's world. He is their Prince. That's why Jesus came to establish a Kingdom–in the world but not of the world. This Kingdom that Christ came to set up, one day will leave this world, with Christ. Our King is in heaven, where we shall be one day, until he cleanses this world of sin and Satan that he might set up his Kingdom on earth.

This is a material world, a physical world, but our God is a spirit and we worship him in spirit and in truth. *(John 4:24)* Since we have been born again, we are now spiritual. The truth is that everything we do is spiritual. That's why you've got to be mindful of what you say and do, because all things are effected by your relationship with God, and your relationship with God effects all things. Ephesians 6:12: *"For we wrestle not against flesh and blood, but against principalities, against powers, against rulers of darkness of this world, against spiritual wickedness in high places."*

Even here in the above passage, we discover that Satan is an organized enemy. He learned to be organized when he was yet with God. In heaven there were cherubim and seraphim. But now he is in charge of a host that includes principalities, that are superior in rank to Powers. That's why we need to rightly divide the word of truth, that we may be able to resist the devil when he shows up.

Satan Is Not Satisfied With Past Accomplishments

Jesus tells us up front what the objectives of the enemy are: "The thief cometh not but for to steal and to kill and to destroy: I am come that they might have life and that might have it more abundantly." *(John 10:10)* Although the enemy comes to ultimately destroy, he uses deception to accomplish his mission. He comes to kill, but you won't see a gun. Oh yes, the way that he persuades unwatchful souls is to appear to bring life.

As you read I Peter 5:8, you will see that Satan not only is busy ruling what he has, but he is also on the prowl. He is not like a lot of us. He wants to see growth in his Kingdom. If you haven't met him since you met Christ, don't think he's not near. Listen to what Peter says: "*Be sober, be vigilant, because your adversary the devil, as a roaring lion walketh about seeking whom he may devour*."

I have often said that the reason why students of the Word should be able to recognize the devil and his tactics is because his tricks are not new!

The three tricks that he attempted upon Christ are the same old tricks that he uses today.

#1) <u>Change these stones to bread.</u>
Selfishness
Jesus never worked a miracle for himself.

#2) <u>Cast Yourself down from this high place</u>.
Self-Destructive
Jesus came not to destroy, but sacrifice himself.

#3) <u>Bow down to me</u>.
Surrender
Jesus understood that his life belonged only to the Father.

<u>Satan Is Destined to the Lake of Fire</u>

Satan is truly a fool! He thinks that his power is absolute. What he doesn't know is that all he has done was simply allowed to be done by God. You know how there are those who think that they are in charge–no one can tell them any thing. They think they know it all. Satan meant it all for evil, but God is going to turn it all for our good.

Look at II Thessalonians 2:7-8 "*For the mystery of iniquity doth already work: only he who now letteth will let, until he be taken out of the way. And then shall that wicked be revealed, whom the Lord shall consume with the spirit of his mouth, and shall destroy with the brightness of his coming.*"

Satan may be riding high today, but don't let any of that fool you. Satan's days are numbered. And you should also know that we are not waiting for him to be defeated at this time, thousand years ago Jesus said "I beheld Satan as lighting fall from heaven." Not only that, but also when Jesus died and rose from the dead, He announced that all power in heaven and in earth was in his hand. Satan is already defeated. He is just trying to take down as many as he can before God has completed His will.

But the final outcome is Revelation 20:10: "And the devil that deceived them was cast into the **lake of fire** (this is worse than Hell) and brimstone, where the beast and the false prophet are, and shall be tormented day and night for ever and ever." Oh, and look at verses 14-15 also: "And death and hell were cast into the lake of fire. This is the second death. And whosoever was not found written in the book of life was cast into the lake of fire." I'm sure that this includes the one third of the angelic host that fell with Satan.

Oh, yes! That's good news to the soul. One of these days we won't have to be tempted and accused by the devil any longer. We will live with our loved ones; saints of the past, present, and future; the faithful angels; and the Lord Jesus Christ our God. Amen!

BIBLIOGRAPHY

Unger, Merrill F., The Unger's Bible Dictionary.
Chicago: Moody Press, 1966

Dake, Finis J., The Dake's Annotated Reference Bible.
Lawrenceville: Dake Bible Sales, Inc., 1963.